# Tea
# on Prayer

# The Christian Tradition

by Fr Robert Taylerson

*All booklets are published thanks to the*
*generous support of the members of the*
*Catholic Truth Society*

CATHOLIC TRUTH SOCIETY
PUBLISHERS TO THE HOLY SEE

# Contents

Some of the material used in this book has been previously used in a course handbook on Christian Prayer. Permission has been given by St Mary's College Oscott to use copyright material from the DFP course-book 'D1.8 Prayer and the Spiritual Writers of the Catholic Tradition' (Oscott 2006).

# Introduction

**Different Christian understandings of "prayer"**

Why is there more than one definition of prayer? The *Catechism of the Catholic Church* (CCC) and other catechetical works, present many understandings from our Christian history.

### Prayer words in the New Testament Greek

Most writers of the first Christian centuries when writing about prayer have, in their minds meanings which come from the literal understanding of the New Testament Greek prayer words (*proseuche, deesis, euche, erotao*) which contain a strong sense of "to ask God for something." For Christian writers of the second millennium, however, the understanding of prayer broadened, sometimes to the extent that some of the original New Testament meanings of the word "prayer" were overlooked.

### New and old definitions

When I was young I was taught from the *"Penny Catechism"* in primary school. To the question "What is prayer?" the reply was "Prayer is the raising up of the mind and heart to God". This "answer" comes from the writings of St John Damascene who lived in Jerusalem in the late seventh and early eighth century.

Paragraph 2559 of the CCC, however, gives John Damascene's full starting sentence, "Prayer is the raising-up of one's mind and heart to God or the requesting of good things from God". Here we can see a fuller picture of the concepts of prayer in the Greek-speaking world at the time. John Damascene's quote comes in the work in which he attempts to express the teachings of the main Greek writers to date. In reading beyond his first sentence we see that this is the start of a discussion on prayer, which is more a reflection than a definition; "Prayer is an uprising of the mind to God or a petitioning of God for what is good. How then did it happen that our Lord offered up prayer in the case of Lazarus, and at the hour of His passion? For His holy mind was in no need either of any uprising towards God...." and so on.

The CCC definition does include "requesting of good things from God", which was the prominent understanding in the early Church, (but absent from the *"Penny Catechism"* ), but even this more complete "definition" is not the final answer, but just a starting point for reflection. Damascene's words in the CCC are for us too, a starting-point for reflection, and an invitation into a deeper mystery, not "the final answer".

The CCC includes more "modern definitions" too. In paragraph 2558 we have Thérèse of Lisieux's words: "For me, prayer is a surge of the heart; it is a simple look turned towards heaven, it is a cry of recognition and love, embracing both trial and joy." We realise that her nineteenth century Carmelite tradition uses a still broader understanding of "prayer". Many Christians in our world today feel more at home with this definition than with Damascene's.

## "Prayer" in this book

The chapters of this book look at a selection of Christian writers on prayer. They includes some details on the practice of prayer, some on the theology of prayer, some on the words or attitudes used in prayer, and some explanations of the terminology of prayer. The book is presented in an historical framework. Partly for brevity's sake and partly because modern writers tend to develop rather than innovate ideas on prayer, the book concentrates on the first sixteen hundred Christian years.

Inevitably it is a personal selection, and is not comprehensive. I am a tutor for the Diaconate formation programme at St Mary's College, Oscott, where I teach a course on prayer.

# The First Christian Latin Writers on Prayer

## Tertullian & Cyprian

### *Tertullian*

Quintus Septimus Florens Tertullian was born in the African part of the Roman Empire, in Carthage in 160 AD. His father was a Centurian for the Roman proconsul there. Tertullian became a lawyer, then converted to Christianity in 193 AD, quickly becoming a priest and Christian author. Towards the end of his life he joined a very strict sect, the Montanists, criticised the Pope (Callistus) for being prepared to forgive adultery and fornication, and fell out with the Catholic Church. His early works, (including his writings on prayer) however, have always been held in high esteem. He wrote the first teaching document on prayer that we know of in the Christian Church.

# A new form of prayer

In Tertullian's introduction to the "Our Father" (the "Lord's Prayer") he describes it as a "new form of prayer" which needs to be like "new wine in new wineskins." It is the culmination of the promises. Tertullian describes the praying of the Our Father as heavenly rather than earthly and encourages the practice of praying it secretly, with modest confidence in the prayer. He acclaims its brevity and sees it as a compressed source of much spiritual life; "...for it has embraced not only the special duties of prayer, be it veneration of God or petition of man, but almost every discourse of the Lord, every record of His discipline; so that, if fact the prayer comprises an epitome of the whole Gospel."

It has long been a tradition in Christianity to give those who are learning about Christ a copy of the "Our Father". Starting from his description of the Our Father as "the epitome of the whole gospel," Tertullian was the first Christian writer to use this text to explain the rest of the gospel and to outline the Christian faith. He taught the Our Father as the "foundation of further desires" encouraging all to examine and reflect on the content and sequence of the petitions in the Our Father, to consider what should be desired and requested from God by the Christian.

## We are part of what we pray for

He is keen that his readers understand that as we pray we are part of the prayed-for outcome, i.e., he wants God's name to be hallowed **in us**, God's kingdom to come **in us**, God's will to be done **in us**. He is keen that we reflect on other passages of scripture to deepen our understanding. Tertullian suggests that it is through the Church that the names "Father" and "Son" have meaning. Through this one name of "Father" therefore we and all who belong to his family give honour to God. He reminds us that God did not make known the name "Father" to Moses when Moses asked his name, nor to anyone else.

Tertullian continues his reflections on all the petitions of the Our Father in similar vein. According to Tertullian after the things of heaven (his name, his will, his kingdom,) God then allows us to ask for what we need in this present world. "Let your first care be for the kingdom of God and all these other things will be given to you." (*Mt* 6:33).

## Daily Bread

For Tertullian the request for daily bread is not only practical but also spiritual. It asks for Christ who is the "bread of life" (*Jn* 6:35). He reminds us that the "bread is the word of the living God who has come down from heaven" (*Jn* 6:31) and that Christ's body is seen in (what

9

appears to be) bread; "This is my body" (*Lk* 22:19). For Tertullian, asking for our daily bread is asking to live with Christ and be one body with him.

Tertullian reminds us that the man who knocked on his friend's door in the middle of the night was looking for bread (*Lk* 11:5) and that the prayer "Give us **this** day" might be echoed in the scriptural precept "Do not be anxious about what you will eat tomorrow" (*Mt* 6:34). Caring only for the needs of this day is emphasised by his reference to the gospel story of the man who had great harvests and wanted to store them and live in security, but died that night (*Lk* 12:16-21).

## General teaching on prayer

*Praying at all times*

Tertullian looks at good prayer habits, encouraging kneeling at prayer and praying "at all times". (this phrase Tertullian interprets as praying wherever we get the opportunity). He recommends fixed times for prayer, at least three times a day (9.00am, 12.00 noon and 3.00pm), in addition to the prayers of morning and evening, which he sees as a sacred duty. He encourages Christians to pray before they eat and even before they have a bath! "The refreshment and food of the spirit come before the needs of the body: the things of heaven come before those of earth."

Tertullian also looks at practices which were common, or in dispute in his day, trying to see how the traditions developed, and assessing what use they might be to the community, or to individuals. He looks at such traditions as the washing of hands, taking off cloaks before prayer, sitting after prayer, the lifting of hands in prayer, the kiss of peace, the tradition of the Stations (commemoration days of martyrs kept in their churches), the dress of women and whether virgins should dress differently from married women, of prayers to be said when welcoming brother or sister Christians etc.

In Chapter twenty seven of Tertullian's work he encourages the prayer of the Our Father to be expanded by the use of psalms or phrases of psalms and by alleluias. He sees these enhancements to prayer as increasing its praise and reverence and making it, "fit to be offered as a very pleasing sacrifice".

## Prayer and sacrifice

Tertullian's work is completed (in Chapters 28 and 29) by first directing our understanding of prayer to see it as an offering of the spirit which does away with earlier sacrifices. He quotes Isaiah 1:11: "I am tired of the blood of bulls and sheep and goats. Who asked you to bring all this when you come and worship me?"

Tertullian asks what God really wants, and directs us to John's gospel "The hour is coming, Jesus says, when those who truly worship God will worship him in spirit and in truth. For God is Spirit" (*Jn* 4:23-24).

Tertullian sees all who pray as having a priestly function (offering sacrifice):

> "We are the true worshippers in spirit and the true priests: praying in the spirit, we make our sacrifice of prayer in spirit, an offering which is God's own and acceptable to him. This is the offering which he asked for, and which he has provided for himself. This is the sacrifice offered from the heart, fed on faith, prepared by faith, unblemished in innocence, pure in chastity, garlanded with love, which we must bring to God's altar, in a procession of good works, to the accompaniment of psalms and hymns. It will obtain for us from God all that we ask."

## Conclusion ... the effects of prayer

In his concluding encouragement to pray, in Chapter twenty nine, Tertullian lists some of the effects of prayer:

> "...to call back the souls of the deceased from the very highway of death, to straighten the feeble, to heal the sick, to cleanse the devil-possessed, to open the bars of the prison, to loose the hands of the innocent. It also absolves sin, drives back

temptations, quenches persecutions, strengthens the weak-hearted, delights the high-minded, brings home wayfarers, stills the waves, confounds robbers, feeds the poor, rules the rich, lifts up the fallen, supports the unstable, upholds them that stand."

---

### Cyprian

The second Latin writer on prayer was St Cyprian, bishop of Carthage and martyr. Cyprian was born in approximately 200 AD of wealthy African parents and trained in rhetoric (public speaking) for which he became well-famed. In the year 246 he converted to Christianity, and rapidly became priest, then bishop by the year 249. His episcopate had many difficulties which included Decian's persecution of Christians and the plague, which also killed many. Cyprian himself was beheaded in Valerian's persecution in the year 258.

---

### New man saying "Father"

Like Tertullian, Cyprian wrote on prayer using the "Our Father" as his model. Much of Tertullian's teaching was repeated by Cyprian. Some teachings, however, were different. Cyprian had a clearer association of baptism with the Our Father than did Tertullian. He described the one who is baptised as the "new man" who "says 'Father' first of all". In reflecting on "Give us this day our daily bread" Cyprian looks to God himself, the father who gives us life, as the feeder and the food for those who commit their lives to him:

"To those who seek the kingdom of God and his righteousness, he has promised to give all else besides. Since everything indeed belongs to God, he who possesses God wants for nothing, if he himself is not found wanting before God".

## Scripture and prayer

Cyprian said: "Be constant in prayer as in reading; now speak to God; now let God speak to you". In this he both formulated one of the first directives of spiritual reading of scripture and described a unity of prayer and scripture reading which was cherished by Christians from then on.

## Prayer for sanctification

Cyprian also took up Tertullian's understanding of the kingdom of God coming "in us" by encouraging daily prayer for our sanctification.

## Concluding reflections

Tertullian's text is a starting-point for reflection on the nature of prayer, the teaching of prayer, and the development of habits of prayer. It also starts to gently explore some theological questions about prayer What is its purpose? What might be meant by "praying at all times"? What is the point of praying that "God's will be done?" In reflecting on the phrase "Our Father", Tertullian develops a concept of Church as family, and so sees prayer as a community activity. The community of earth and heaven is associated with God by "family-type" bonds. In addition to seeing prayer as petition (and seeing nothing wrong with asking God for whatever seems good), Tertullian sees prayer in some measure as replacing Old Testament sacrifice.

For Cyprian, the man made new in baptism seeks his Father, God, through the precepts of the Our Father. He expects our greatest desire, expressed in prayer, to be for God. He commends us to pray daily to be made holy, and sees reflective scripture reading and prayer as being hand-in-hand in the Christian life.

# The First Christian Greek Writers on Prayer

## Origen, Ignatius and Others

### Earliest Greek writers

The earliest Greek-language writer on prayer mentioned in the *Catechism of the Catholic Church* is Ignatius of Antioch (d. 107 AD). CCC 2837 recalls his letter to the Ephesians, where he sees the Eucharist as being the "daily bread" of the Our Father. The Our Father also figures in the *Didache*, a Greek text of uncertain origin, but which may well have been written before 120 AD. It indicates that a doxology (an additional phrase which gives glory to God) "for yours are the power and the glory for ever", was already commonly being added to the Our Father. However, by far the most important early writer in Greek on prayer was Origen. It is to him that we now turn our attention.

### *Origen*

Origen lived from 185 to 254 AD. He was a follower of the theologian and catechist, St Clement of Alexandria (and elements of Origen's teaching came from Clement). At the age of 18 he succeeded Clement as head of the catechetical school in Alexandria. He wrote texts on scripture, recognising literal, moral and allegorical meanings. He had a creativity as a mystical writer which later writers have imitated, extending the use of allegory very widely.

Not all of his teaching met with Church approval, and some of his theology has been condemned as relying more on philosophy than on scripture. All of his teachings on prayer, however, are well used and highly respected. His work *De Oratione* (= De Orat. "On Prayer") is the first Christian text which attempts to develop a theology of prayer.

## On Prayer

Origen starts by assuming that we don't know how to pray well. He quotes St Paul, saying that we do not pray as we ought (*Rm* 8:26). How, asks Origen, can we pray as we ought if we do not know what we should pray for? He looks at scripture: Pray for those who abuse you (*Lk* 6:28). Pray the Lord of the harvest to send labourers to the harvest (*Mt* 9:38; *Lk* 10:2). Pray that you may not enter into temptation (*Lk* 22:40; *Mt* 26:41, *Mk* 14:38). He also notes that "So if you are offering a gift at the altar, and then remember that your brother has something against you, leave your gift there before the altar and go, first be reconciled …" (*Mt* 5:23-24). To Origen it is clear that prayer takes on different forms in different circumstances. His questioning mind enables him to hold several models of prayer at once, or to raise several questions concerning prayer at once. This gives a breadth to his writings on prayer and prompts his use of allegory.

## Pray and vow

In biblical Greek the word *euche* means either "prayer" or "sacred vow". When Origen looks at the words for prayer in scripture he finds the first mention in the passage where Jacob takes flight to Mesopotamia (*Gn* 28:20-22). In modern English versions of this passage (e.g. *The New Jerusalem Bible*) the word *euche* is translated not as "prayer" but as "vow". Origen seems to quote both from the Hebrew and the Septuagint (the Hebrew bible translated into Greek). Origen wrestles with the different meanings of words for prayer/vow to good effect.

Although the double meaning is not present in our English prayer words, it is still good to ask God to oversee the solemn promises which we make today. They too can be sacred and prayerful.

## What is the purpose of asking in prayer?

In the fifth chapter of his book Origen acknowledges that some people find prayer superfluous. He knows that most people who believe in God value prayer highly. He first tries to present clearly the arguments of those who find prayer superfluous (in order to develop a theology which overcomes them). These arguments are:

i.   God has foreknowledge. What is the use of prayer when he knows what we need better than we do?

ii.  God determines much in advance. It would be foolish for us to pray for the sun to rise. Likewise, he who prays for the summer sun to stop shining because he is too hot is mad. How do we know that much prayer is not madness?

iii. Two texts of scripture seem to contradict each other, but together raise further questions about the purpose of prayer:

*(a)* some (sinners) are "estranged from the womb" (*Ps* 57[58]:3) and...

*(b)* others (righteous) set apart form their mother's womb (cf. *Ga* 1:15). Some argue, says Origen, that, if you are "estranged", prayer will not change that, and, if you are "set apart" good things will happen whether or not you pray.

iv. Those to be saved in Christ, according to Ephesians 1:3-5 have been chosen "In him (Christ) before the foundation of the world that they should be holy and blameless before him." Origen recalls this text to pose the question; "What is the point of prayer?"

Origen's reply to these arguments looks first at the theological understanding of freedom. He uses the analogy of "movement" to reflect on "freedom". He compares three types of movement. He uses the example of a stone as an inanimate object. He uses the example of a plant as his first animate object. His third object for comparison of movement is a human being. Origen compares the three. He recognises different limitations on movement, and by analogy, limitations to freedom. He argues that human beings have a fuller freedom, which comes from within themselves, whereas the freedom of other objects is limited.

Having concluded that human beings have freedom in what they do, he then suggests that God's foreknowledge includes knowledge of those human choices made from such personal freedom. God's choices do not contradict human freedom, but work with it. i.e. God is aware of prayer which has yet to be prayed. God knows of the prayer beforehand and has already taken it into account in his decisions.

With regard to "praying for the sun to rise", Origen describes the lesser freedom that the sun has, and encourages us to use prayer for those with greater freedom (human beings), while not decrying prayer for natural phenomena.

With regard to praying "constantly" (1 *Th* 5:17) Origen sees deeds of virtue as fulfilling this precept. The CCC uses this idea of Origen's when it describes prayer and Christian life as inseparable. Origen also urges us to move from praying for little things to praying for ever greater things.

Next Origen looks at the passage in 1 Timothy 2:1 "I urge that supplications, prayers, intercessions, and thanksgivings be made for all men." This association in 1 Timothy gives rise to Origen's ideas that these are different parts of a praying process, which should each be used appropriately.

He discusses whether we should pray to Jesus or to the Father and reminds us that Jesus himself taught us to pray to the Father. Origen concludes (using imagery of bride and bridegroom) by encouraging us to seek the deepest beauty of the things of heaven and of God.

Although his teaching on prayer is neither complete nor foolproof, Origen's works are important. His fertile mind has, in these initial endeavours to understand the nature of prayer, given us an introductory theology of prayer and set us on trains of thought which are still fruitful today.

## Origin's teaching on the "Our Father"

*Our Father who art in Heaven*

Origen looks for Old Testament references to the Father, and like Tertullian, finds none in Old Testament prayers. He does state, however, that God is seen as a father and those who draw near to him are like sons e.g. in Deuteronomy 32:18 "You have deserted God who begot you and have forgotten God who nourishes you." Like Tertullian he sees Jesus as revealing God as Father to us, quoting both Paul and John (*Rm* 8:15, *Jn* 1:12) and encouraging our spirit of sonship. "Our life", says Origen, "should be a constant prayer in which we say 'Our Father in heaven' ".

Origen stresses the distinction between God-the-creator and all else as creation. Holding this thought in prayer helps us to address God as he really is, above all creation.

## Hallowed be Thy Name

Origen starts by implying that the name has not already been fully hallowed. He looks at name changes Abram/Abraham Saul/Paul Simon/Peter. He then sees God's name as "I am" before Jesus called him "Father" and so God also has had a name-change. He draws on scripture texts such as "They will remember your name in all generations" (*Ps* 44[45]:17). Origen reads "Hallowed be thy name" as an imperative (something which must be done), i.e., the hallowing of God's name is an uncompleted task which we are to pursue. The name change from "I am" to "Father" evoked by Origen's reflections is for us, too, a focus of reflection in prayer.

## Thy Kingdom Come

Origen's teaches that the Kingdom of God is within us. It is a kingdom without partnerships. Origen writes that there should be:

> "no partnership between righteousness and iniquity, no fellowship of light with darkness, no accord of

Christ with Belial, so the kingdom of sin cannot coexist with the kingdom of God. Both sin and death need to be destroyed in us that we grow in the life of the blessings of rebirth and resurrection."

## *Thy Will be Done on Earth as it is in Heaven*

The *Catechism of the Catholic Church* quotes Origen when it says that "in committing ourselves to Christ we can become one spirit with him, and thereby accomplish his will, in such wise that it will be perfect on earth as it is in heaven."

## *Give us this Day our Daily Bread*

Origen does not see this as requesting things to eat in an earthly sense. He quotes four phrases from John's gospel which speak of food or bread in different ways:

John 6:26 "(You) seek me not because you saw signs, but because you ate your fill of loaves" and (*Jn* 6:27). "do not labour for food that perishes, but for the food that endures to eternal life, which the Son of Man will give you" He goes on to remind us (*Jn* 6:51) that Jesus is the "bread of life" and concludes with John 6:53-57, "Unless you eat the flesh of the Son of man you can not have life within you."

Through his reflection on these texts he concludes that we should pray for Christ's presence in our lives to the fullest, rather than simply for material food.

Origen then looks at the Greek backgrounds for the word "daily" (*epiousion*) before coming to his conclusion:

"The living bread which comes down from heaven and is distributed to the mind and the soul gives a share in its own power to the person who provides himself food from it. And thus the bread we ask will be 'daily' in the sense that it will be 'for our being.' Moreover, just as the person nourished becomes empowered in differing ways according to the quality of the food, which may be solid and suitable for athletes or like milk and vegetables, so also it follows that the Word of God is given either as milk suitable for children or as vegetables fit for the sick or as meat special for those who are taking part in contests."

Origen proceeds to advise us to pray for this daily bread. We should also pray to be made worthy of it.

## Special directions

Like Tertullian, Origen next concerns himself with the "how", "when", "where" habits of customary prayer. He relies much on St Paul. "Paul... describes the disposition and says that we must pray, "without anger or quarrelling"; and he describes the posture by the phrase "lifting holy hands" (1 *Tm* 2:8). Origen concludes,

"...the person who is about to come to prayer should withdraw for a little while and prepare himself, and so become more attentive and active for the whole of prayer. He should cast away all temptations and troubling thoughts and remind himself so far as he is able of the Majesty whom he approaches and that it is impious to approach Him carelessly, sluggishly, and disdainfully; and he should put away all extraneous things. This is how he should come to prayer, stretching out his soul, as it were, instead of his hands, straining his mind toward God instead of his eyes, raising his governing reasoning from the ground and standing it before the Lord instead of standing."

## Origen's allegory

This last phrase shows well the extent of Origen's allegory as he imagines our "reasoning" standing rather than simply our bodies standing! It also finds an echo the start of John Damascene's teaching on prayer, "Prayer is the raising up of one's mind and heart to God or the requesting of good things from God", written some four centuries later. Origen's advice is on the technique of praying, albeit using allegorical language, whereas Damascene's words are on the nature of prayer. An earlier writer's comments on technique, or allegories of the activity of prayer have been used by a later writer to define the nature of prayer.

## Origen's other works

One passage of Origen's scripture commentary on the Song of Songs is well worth a mention because it gave rise to a view of spiritual life in the Middle Ages and greatly influenced future views on prayer as a result.

Halfway through the prologue to this commentary Origen wonders why the books attributed to Solomon (i.e. Proverbs, Ecclesiastes and Song of Songs) are in the order we receive them in the bible....

"... he (Solomon) first taught in Proverbs the subject of morals, setting regulations for life together as was fitting, in concise and brief maxims. And he included the second subject, which is called the natural discipline, in Ecclesiastes, in which he discusses many natural things.... He also handed down the subject of contemplation in the ... Song of Songs, in which he urges upon the soul the love of the heavenly and the divine under the figure of the bride and the bridegroom, teaching us that we must attain fellowship with God by the paths of loving affection and love."

Origen's reflections laid the path for later mystical writers to suggest a "type" of spiritual progress in Christian's lives. This progress is often seen as having three stages, similar to Origen's progress from Proverbs to Ecclesiastes to Song of Songs.

*Stage One*: One's central attention being on moral aspects, (right and wrong, being free from sin) at an early stage of spiritual Progress,

*Stage Two*: Looking at the realities of this world and the mysteries of God in their true light,

*Stage Three*: Growing in the personal love of God, in the model of attention and love typified by bride/ bridegroom relationship.

## Concluding reflections

In the Greek-speaking world of the early Church the *Didache* shows the early practice of adding a doxology (giving of glory to God) to the end of the Our Father when used in daily prayer.

The great early writer in Greek on prayer is Origen. His approach is to see prayer as more mystery than process. It is always deeper than it first appears. In terms of "praying at all times", Origen sees anything virtuous as fulfilling this precept. He sees prayer as an exercise of freedom and suggests that it has its profound effects in free human beings. God's foreknowledge and plan takes prayer into account.

Origen's reflections on 1 Timothy 2:1 "I urge that supplications, prayers, intercessions, and thanksgivings be made for all." give rise to his idea that these are different parts of a praying process. In terms of "what to ask for in prayer", unlike Tertullian, Origen steers us away from praying for small everyday things towards praying for great things. In his reflections on scriptural books attributed to Solomon, Origen suggested a model of Christian spiritual progress, which would be used by later writers to form a spiritual theology and practice of prayer.

# East and West in the Fourth & Fifth Century

## Cyril of Jerusalem, Gregory of Nyssa, Augustine and Prosper of Aquitaine

As the years pass in the Christian tradition, so writers on prayer come from more diverse cultures and traditions. Fourth and fifth century writers give a wider range of understandings than their predecessors. The writers which we consider in this chapter are key to their era, and each contributes something important to Christian teaching on prayer. To understand this period fully, however, many more writers would need to be taken into account.

## *Cyril of Jerusalem*

Cyril was born in Palestine in 313 AD and educated in Jerusalem. He was ordained priest around the year 345. When the bishop of Jerusalem died in 348, Cyril was consecrated bishop in his place. He had a difficult episcopate, being expelled three times from his see, but eventually in the late 370s returned to a more peaceful Jerusalem, and continued in peace. He wrote in Greek. He is quoted in the CCC with his reflection on the "Amen" in the Our Father, saying that it "ratifies what God has taught us". His focus, in this way, on each and every word, accompanied his quest to understand and explain it fully. Much of his writing, however, is of a mystical style, containing allegory and symbolism.

## Allegory and symbolism

Cyril develops Origen's allegory and symbolism. The CCC uses a quote typical of Cyril's in reflecting on the phrase "who art in heaven". Cyril takes our perception deeper than seeing heaven simply as a place. He calls us to see heaven in those who are holy, "Heaven could also be those who bear the image of the heavenly world, and in whom God dwells and tarries."

## Broad understanding of prayer

Cyril's instinct seems to be to broaden the understanding of prayer, to associate it with all Christian life, "It is not tied down to a fixed timetable, rather it is a state which endures by night and day. Our soul should be directed in God, not merely when we think of prayer, but even when we are concerned with something else". He likes to express it as including desire for God and devotion: "You should not think of prayer as being a matter of words. It is a desire for God, an indescribable devotion, not of human origin, but the gift of God's grace."

With Cyril, the understanding of prayer in the Greek-speaking churches starts to be seen as a spiritual state, a desire of holy men and women, rather than simply an activity.

---

### *Gregory of Nyssa*

A trio of mystical theologians from Cappadocia taught in the mid fourth century. They were Basil [the Great], Gregory of Nazianzus, and Gregory of Nyssa.

Gregory of Nyssa (c. 330-395) studied in Caesarea, Constantinople and Athens. He then journeyed through Syria and Egypt to experience different monastic practices. He was friends with

---

Gregory of Nazianzus (329- 390) with whom he had been a student. Together they published selections from Origen and also formed a monastic rule. Each became a bishop and wrote widely on theology. Gregory of Nyssa was also the younger brother of Basil (329-379), who like him became a monk, then a bishop. The three are often referred to as the "Cappadocian Fathers" and their preaching and theology renewed the church in their age. All three taught on prayer. Basil is quoted in the CCC section on prayer, as is Gregory of Nazianzus, but, for me Gregory of Nyssa is the central teacher on prayer, especially with his five sermons on the Lord's Prayer.

## What is prayer?

In the introduction to his teachings on the Lord's Prayer, Gregory says:

> "Prayer is intimacy with God and contemplation of the invisible. It satisfies our yearnings and makes us equal to the angels. Through it good prospers, evil is destroyed and sinners will be converted. Prayer is the enjoyment of things present and the substance of things to come."

Gregory makes a new distinction between the Greek words *euche* and *proseuche*. "A vow (*euche*) is the promise of something consecrated to the service of God; whereas prayer (*proseuche*) is the offering to God of a supplication for good things". Gregory follows and expands the mystical teaching of Origen on prayer. Whenever he comes up with an idea of what prayer is, he realises that the idea is incomplete, and so as his work progresses more and more images are given. The more he reflects on the "Our Father" and on prayer in general, the richer and more varied his images become. He commends us also to contemplate God's beauty, "We must contemplate the beauty of the Father without ceasing and adorn our own souls accordingly".

## THE WEST

### Augustine

There are two well-know saints named Augustine, of Canterbury and of Hippo. The writer on prayer is St Augustine of Hippo. He lived from 354 to 430 and wrote a lot! His best-known works are his "*Confessions*" and his "*City of God*", though most of his writings on prayer are not found in these. He wrote a letter to Proba, a rich widow, on praying the "Our Father". He also talked about prayer in many of his sermons and in his scripture commentaries, particularly those on the Psalms, on his reflections on Matthew's Gospel in general and his reflections on the Sermon on the Mount.

## From the commentary on the Sermon on the Mount

*Give us this day our Daily Bread*

The CCC quotes from Augustine's Commentary on the Sermon on The Mount:

"The Eucharist is our daily bread. The power belonging to this divine food makes it a bond of union. Its effect is then understood as unity, so that, gathered into his Body and made members of him, we may become what we receive... This also is our daily bread: the readings you hear each day in church and the hymns you hear and sing. All these are necessities for our pilgrimage.

Augustine's "daily bread" reflection is broad. Like Tertullian he considers "this day" in terms of Christ's teaching that we do not labour for things for tomorrow (*Mt* 6:34). He considers Eastern Churches, which lack the tradition of daily Eucharist, and also looks at the norm of praying the Our Father after we have already received the Eucharist that day. He comes to the conclusion that there are three valid daily requests, for:

i.   the bread necessary for the body,

ii.  for that visible hallowed bread (Eucharist) and

iii. for the invisible bread of the word of God.

*Forgive us our Debts as we Forgive our Debtors*

Augustine remembers Christ's words that we are to pray for our enemies, so he sees forgiveness too as going beyond those who ask pardon. He concludes:

> "By no possibility, however, could one truthfully say that he prays for one he has not pardoned. And therefore we must confess that all the sins that are committed against us are to be forgiven, if we wish those to be forgiven by our Father which we commit against Him."

## General comments

According to Augustine the "Our Father" is both for this present world and for the world to come. The seven petitions of the prayer mirror the seven-fold structure he sees in the Sermon on the Mount as a whole. He see them as and bringing unity between this world and the next.

# Augustine's letter to Proba

Proba was very rich and very powerful, the widow of the wealthiest man in the Roman Empire. Three of her sons had been consul. When Rome was pillaged in the year 410 AD she moved to Carthage in North Africa, and there she founded a community of religious women.

When Augustine sets out to respond to her letter asking how to pray, he has an unusual task. Imagine yourself getting such a letter from someone very wealthy (e.g., Bill Gates), or someone used to having had much power (e.g., Margaret Thatcher), asking for teaching on prayer. How would you respond?

Augustine spends a lot of his letter discussing the correct disposition for prayer. The CCC gives two quotes from Augustine's letter to Proba:

Paragraph 2762 of the CCC, quotes Augustine's words, reminiscent of Tertullian, "Run through all the words of the holy prayers [in scripture], and I do not think that you will find anything in them not contained and included in the Lord's Prayer".

## Prayer and desire

Augustine talks about human desire: "God wills that our desire should be exercised in prayer, that we may be able to receive what he is prepared to give." This quote marks one of the key ways in which Augustine broadened the definition of Christian prayer in the West.

*How to pray*

Augustine first asks that Proba see herself in the true state of life of a widow. He bids her see that she has been given time by God for prayer, rather than other duties. He asks her to trust not in her riches, but to see herself as totally dependent on God. Neither friends nor status are to be valued compared with the time shared with God in prayer. Augustine wants Proba to remember the uncertainties of life.

> "... you are a wealthy widow of rank and the mother of an illustrious family. I want you to experience yourself as desolate even while your family remains with you and follows your directions. You have not yet attained that life where consolation is true and certain. ..."

Augustine's first advice in terms of what to pray for is "Pray for a happy life!" Augustine teaches that a happy life does not consist of living just as one wishes. There is not necessarily anything wrong with wanting a particular role in the world, provided that it is desired because of the good it can do. Friendship, too, is an appropriate object of prayer, but the Christian should desire to be friends even with enemies.

Augustine's touchstone concerns preparing ourselves for heaven:

"The life we live in time is wasted if we do not spend it becoming worthy to live in eternity. Everything we can usefully and properly desire must certainly be seen in respect to the one life that is lived with God and that comes from God."

Augustine recommends Proba to desire the blessed life that comes from the Lord. He encourages her to pray a lot, noting that Jesus spent the whole night in prayer. He also counsels against using superfluous words. Praying much, but not using too many words, for Augustine, means having longings, devout stirrings of the heart. "Often the task is carried out more by groaning than by speaking, with more tears than breath". Augustine is redefining the central aspect of prayer in terms of the heart, the longing, the yearning, the attention, rather than using the "right words" or "many words."

*Teachings on the "Our Father"*

The teachings on the words of the "Our Father" and their meanings are summed up succinctly to Proba:

"So when we say, "Hallowed be thy name," we are counselling ourselves to desire that name, which is always holy, may be held holy also among men; that is, that it may not be treated with contempt: and this is for the benefit not of God but of men.

When we say, "Thy Kingdom come," which will certainly come whether we wish it or not, we arouse our desire for that kingdom, that it may come for us, and that we may be worthy to reign therein.

When we say, "Thy will be done on earth as it is in heaven," we are asking him for obedience for ourselves that his will may be done in us as it is done in heaven by his angels.

(Elsewhere Augustine frequently suggests that it is an excellent and necessary practice to pray that we keep his commandments and yearn to keep them.)

When we say, "Give us this day our daily bread," we mean by "today" this present time. We are asking either for sufficiency, by expressing its principal part, signifying the whole by the name "bread"; or for the sacrament of believers, which is necessary at the present time in order to obtain the happiness not of this present time but of eternity.

When we say, "Forgive us our trespasses as we forgive those who trespass against us," we are advising ourselves both as to what we should ask for, and what we should do to be worthy to receive it.

When we say, "Lead us not into temptation," we counsel ourselves to make this petition lest we be abandoned by his help, and either be deceived into consenting to some temptation or be so downcast as to give in to it.

When we say, "Deliver us from evil," we bring ourselves to reflect that we are not yet in that happy state where we shall suffer no evil. This last petition in the Lord's prayer has such a wide scope that a Christian may in any trouble express his pain by it, pour forth his tears, begin from it, linger over it, and end his prayer at this point.

It is necessary by these words to impress the realities themselves on our memory. For whatever other words we may say – whether the devotion of one praying precedes and forms the words to express itself, or accompanies the words and grows from them – if we are praying in the right way, we say nothing that has not already a place in the Lord's Prayer."

### Answering prayer

One further aspect of prayer in the letter to Proba letter is Augustine's teaching about the answering of prayer. Augustine points out that God grants requests to sinners. He gives the example of the devil in the book of Job, whom God allows to bring disasters into Job's life. Another example is the request of the evil spirits that Jesus should send them into the herd of swine. Augustine counsels that we should never become filled with pride when we see our own prayers answered. We should always recognise that God's granting our requests is not necessarily a sign either that what has been asked for is good, or that the one asking is good.

## Other Augustinian teachings on prayer

### Prayer for the dead

In his "Confessions" (book 9) Augustine composes a prayer for his mother, Monica who has died, and encourages his readers to remember Monica in prayer at the altar of God. In the year 424 he wrote a treatise "The Care of the Dead" in reply to a query of bishop Paulinus of Nola. He commends the practice of such prayer and sees it as beneficial.

### Praying without ceasing

Augustine is aware of the Pauline injunction to pray at all times (1 *Th* 5:17) and in various of his writings teaches that what is important is that we never stop desiring or yearning for the things of God.

## Unanswered prayer

In many of his writings Augustine considers prayer which is not immediately answered by God. This teaches us persistence, encourages us to value the things we ask for and deepens our yearning for what is good. We keep on asking for those things which seem to us to be good. Augustine reminds us: "Man is a beggar before God."

## Jesus prays in us

Augustine teaches us in his commentary on Psalm 85 that Jesus prays in us as we pray: "He prays for us as our priest, prays in us as our Head, and is prayed to by us as our God. Therefore let us acknowledge our voice in him and his in us."

Augustine is rightly respected as a prominent teacher of prayer in the early Western Christian tradition.

---

### Prosper of Aquitaine

St Prosper of Aquitaine closely followed Augustine's ideas and teaching. He is thought to have lived from 390-463 AD. His main claim to fame concerning prayer is his teaching of the necessary unity between prayer and belief. The original quote; "the law of prayer determines the law of belief." ("*Ut legem credendi lex statat*

---

> *supplicandi"* or *"legem credendi lex statuat*
> *supplicandi"*) is thought to have come from his
> book *"The Defence of St Augustine"*.

This precept became widely used by theologians when trying to establish if a particular Church's beliefs were orthodox, (in the sense of "sound" i.e. acceptable teaching, regarded as true). The prayers used in their liturgy were examined. If all the prayers, collects, creeds, scriptures, liturgical formulae, etc. used by any particular church are orthodox, then this is strong evidence that the belief of the community of that church is also orthodox. The Latin tag was soon shortened to *"Lex Orandi, Lex Credendi"* (The law of prayer equates to the law of belief). This is seen as Prosper's important axiom and has been widely used in the Church. The CCC teaches it in the section on *Sacraments of the Faith*.

The unity between prayer and understanding was also later taught by St Benedict (d. 546). In his rule concerning the psalms he expresses similar sentiment to Prosper when he says that they should be sung in such a way that "our minds are in harmony with our voices".

## Liturgical prayer

The word "liturgy" usually implies a public act of worship, prayer or sacramental action. When Prosper's idea became widely used, it was initially to do with liturgical prayer. One of the effects of his axiom, however, was to blur the difference between the definition and use of the terms "prayer" and "liturgy".

Sometimes Prosper's axiom has been used in another way, to expect that how we pray or what we pray are determined by our belief. So into the tradition of the Church have come these three suppositions:

i.  Liturgical and Sacramental formulae and rites may all be defined as "prayer".

ii. The words used in liturgy reflect the beliefs of those who share in that liturgy.

iii. Words and phrases used in my prayers express my beliefs and theological understandings.

## Unity of theology and practice of prayer

If we have a theology of God as all-knowing (*omniscient*), then our theology of prayer must fit in with this. We cannot hold a theology of prayer which suggests that a reason for prayer is to let God know about things of which he may be ignorant. Whatever theology of prayer develops must be in accord with the theology which describes God's qualities.

The Christian theology of God also includes an understanding that God is immutable (unchangeable).

Our theology of prayer must be in accord with this. To suggest that the purpose of prayer might be "to twist God's arm so that he would do something he doesn't want to do" could never be a valid Christian theology of prayer.

## Concluding reflections

The fourth century in both East and West saw a broadening understanding of prayer. Cyril of Jerusalem in the East and Augustine in the West both saw desire, rather than words, as being the heart of prayer. Both Cyril and Gregory of Nyssa deepen Origen's use of allegory and also encourage intimacy with God through prayer. Augustine's teaching uses and deepens his predecessors' teaching concerning "What to ask" and "How to ask it", but he gives us new directions, too. He reflects on the "Our Father", on the implication of equality of all as children of God, derived from the words "Our Father". His reflections also shed light on the phrases of the Our Father: daily bread as temporal needs, Eucharist, and God's Word. He teaches on God's demands for forgiveness of those who trespass against us. Augustine includes teachings on praying for the dead, on unanswered prayer, and on why God answers the prayer of those who are not good.

The Latin tag *"Lex Orandi, Lex Credendi"* (The Law

of Belief is the Law of Prayer) is a simplified conclusion of Prosper's reflections that one can know or test the authenticity of prayers used in liturgy by seeing what teachings of faith they presuppose. It gives a tool to help us to sort out "good prayers" from "bad prayers" and draw together reflections on the words of prayer and the truths of faith. It also goes some way towards removing the boundary between what is seen as "Liturgy" and what is seen as "Prayer".

# Monks, Scriptures, Meditation & Contemplation

This chapter examines monastic prayerful reading of scripture texts (*Lectio Divina*).

## Monastic background

Monasteries had always been places of reflection on scripture. Scripture texts were revered, read reflected on and learned by the earliest monks in the Egyptian desert. St John Chrysostom (d. 407) encouraged monks of Constantinople in similar patterns of reading and meditation. John Cassian (d. 435) brought the Eastern monastic tradition to the West. Cassian's ninth and tenth Conferences, both on prayer, which encouraged the use of scripture, were held in high esteem in all monasteries. St Benedict (d. 550) wrote the first great rule for monastic life. In it, in addition to commending meditation/reflection on the scriptures, he also commended the writings of Cassian. St Jerome (d. 420) not only translated the scriptures into Latin (the *Vulgate*), so that more people could read them, but also saw a knowledge of the scriptures as essential: "Ignorance of Scripture is ignorance of Christ".

St Isidore of Seville (d. 630), following Cyprian's ideas, was a great promoter of the reading of scripture in the context of prayer. His key understanding is that when we pray we talk to God; when we read scripture, God talks to us. This scripture reflection with prayer developed hand-in-hand with the structured praying of psalms, canticles and scripture readings in the daily offices (hours) of monasteries and cathedrals. Familiarity with scripture deepened through monastic traditions which included frequent repetition of scriptural texts. In some monastic and cathedral developments the nature of reflection diversified and aspects of "study" were included in the "reflection".

In the second millennium, the "study" aspects of scripture included rational and philosophical ideas from Aristotle. Anselm (d. 1109) helped this trend. The Muslim scholar, Averroes (d. 1198) in Spain re-introduced Aristotelian philosophy to Christian Europe. His commentaries were used by Ss. Albert and Thomas Aquinas. So scholastic theology grew, combining philosophical reflection with scriptural reflection and the developing understanding of God's revelation.

> ### Guigo II and Lectio Divina
>
> Guigo II was the ninth prior of the motherhouse of
> the Carthusian order (The Grand Chartreuse) from
> 1174 to 1180. He is thought to have written the
> *"Ladder of Monks"*, *"Twelve Meditations"*, and his
> *"Meditation on the Magnificat."* His *"Ladder"* in
> particular has had a great influence on subsequent
> prayerful reading of scripture (*Lectio Divina*).

Thanks to Guigo, Bernard of Clairvaux (d. 1153),
William of St Thierry (d. 1148) and other monks,
techniques of scripture-prayer developed. Scripture was
not only to be studied and analysed, but accepted with
the heart as a life-changing power, always new and fresh,
always able to help one's moral life to grow, to deepen
one's love for the Creator, to fend off evil, to enable more
profound immersion in the mysteries of God and to be
used ever more deeply in service of God and neighbour.

## Monasteries, laity and scripture

Monasteries were places where scripture was read.
Sadly for most of the second millennium in the
Catholic tradition it was little read by laity. Until papal
encouragements of the 1950s and 1960s, personal
private reading of scriptures in the vernacular by laity
was discouraged.

This discouragement stems back to the twelfth century. A group of laity in Metz translated the gospels, Paul's letters and the psalms into the vernacular. They met in private and discussed and interpreted various passages of the scriptures, then excluded from their groups any person, lay or priest, who disagreed with their conclusions.

As a result, the pope (Innocent III) in the year 1199 issued a letter which praised their devotion to scripture, but condemned their secret and exclusive gatherings, especially the anti-clericalism which was present. Sadly this led to the synods of Toulouse (in 1229) and Tarragona (in 1234) forbidding the laity to possess or read translations of the Bible in the vernacular.

It was only in the twentieth century that the encouragement to pray and use vernacular translations of scripture in the Catholic Church was once more encouraged. Gradually encouragement grew, until in 1964 the Second Vatican Council issued its Dogmatic Constitution on Divine Revelation (*Dei Verbum*), which encouraged Catholics to read the Bible.

Because many monks could read Latin and often Greek, however, the monastic tradition enabled scripture-based prayer to be a regular component of their life throughout the ages. During the second millennium in the Western Church, scriptural prayer continued to develop in monasteries, but outside of them the growth in prayer was more often in devotions and piety (more of which will be said in the chapter on Friars Prayers and Devotions).

## Guigo's Ladder

Despite restricted access to scripture for lay people elsewhere, Guigo gives a great example of the wholesome use of scripture in monasteries. Guigo introduces his Ladder:

> "One day when I was busy working with my hands I began to think about spiritual work, and all at once four stages of spiritual exercise came into my mind: reading, meditation, prayer and contemplation. These make up a ladder for monks to lift them up from earth to heaven!"

He goes on to give a first description of these rungs:

> "Reading is the careful study of the scriptures, concentrating all one's powers on it. Meditation is the busy application of the mind to seek with the help of one's own reason for knowledge of hidden truth. Prayer is the heart's devoted turning to God to drive away evil and obtain what is good. Contemplation is when the mind is in some sort lifted up to God and held above itself, so that it tastes the joys of everlasting sweetness."

Guigo develops his teaching,

"One precedes the other, not only in the order of time but of causality. Reading comes first, and is, as it were, the foundation; it provides the subject matter we must use for meditation. Meditation considers more carefully what is to be sought after; it digs, as it were for treasure, which it finds and reveals, but since it is not in meditation's power to seize upon the treasure, it directs us to prayer. Prayer lifts itself up to God with all its strength, and begs for the treasure it longs for, which is the sweetness of contemplation. Contemplation, when it comes, rewards the labours of the other three; it inebriates the thirsting soul with the dew of heavenly sweetness. Reading is an exercise of the outward senses; meditation is concerned with the inward understanding; prayer is concerned with desire; contemplation outstrips every faculty. The first degree is proper to beginners, the second to proficients, the third to devotees, the fourth to the blessed."

In the fourteenth paragraph of his work, Guigo stresses the interlinking of the four rungs:

"...reading without meditation is sterile, meditation without reading is liable to error, prayer without meditation is lukewarm, meditation without prayer is unfruitful, prayer when it is fervent wins contemplation, but to obtain it without prayer would be rare, even miraculous."

His work is a short, but classic text, which has been used greatly in the last eight hundred and fifty years. In the late twentieth century, the practice of *Lectio Divina* in a simple form has been revived and given a new impetus. In addition to Guigo's four rungs, which are taken as the starting-point for much *Lectio Divina*, a fifth rung is usually added for those who live in the world. The fifth rung is *"Actio"*, Christian action.

## For Guigo, What is Prayer?

The frequent references to "heart" and "desire", "devoted", "fervent" or "lukewarm", and the sense of the importance of yearning in Guigo's text indicate that his use of the word was based on Augustine's sense of prayer. Guigo is also firmly in the tradition that prayer is an "ascent". The sense that "God is in heaven" and that "heaven is above" disposes Guigo among many to define prayer in terms of moving upwards.

In Guigo's sentence, "The first degree is proper to beginners, the second to proficients, the third to devotees, the fourth to the blessed." he envisages a journey of spiritual life where, at its different stages, different activities or elements will be prevalent. In this he echoes the idea of a personal spiritual journey which we have seen in Origen's commentary on the Song of Songs, but adds his own imagery too.

## A further note on the word "Meditation"

Today the word "meditation" has multiple meanings. One can speak of a piece of music or a work of art as a meditation. It is used to describe interiorisation techniques of Zen Buddhism, of Yoga or reflection on Islamic texts. One can use the adjective "meditative" of a way of life, and talk in general about communities of prayer as meditative. One can use it (as one can the word "contemplative") as a contrast to "active" when talking about styles of religious life.

In the New Testament, words which may be translated as "meditation" are rare. Luke 21:14 uses "praemeditari". In 1 Timothy 4:15, Paul asks his disciple to "take to heart" scripture lessons. Mary's "keeping/storing-up in her heart (*Lk* 2:19, 51) has often been seen as meditation. These examples are present, but do not give clear evidence of widespread practice of what we would recognise as meditation.

Early monastic uses tend to concentrate on "repeating, or ruminating on the Word of God". Augustine several times suggests "When you read or listen you eat: when you meditate you come to understand what you read or hear; you ruminate like an animal."

For the first five hundred years of the Christian tradition all people who read scripture did so aloud. Meditation would be noisy. After this era silent reading became the norm and meditation became quiet.

In the Middle Ages there was more of a sense of using one's reason as part of meditation. This started with St Anselm (d. 1109), was strongly influenced by Hugh of St Victor (d. 1141), and undoubtedly influenced Guigo II and his contemporaries. Further changes of meaning took place after Guigo.

## A note on the word "Contemplation"

The word "contemplation" is not present in scripture, but was common in early philosophy in the Greek language. It was introduced into Christian vocabulary by Clement of Alexandria (d. before 215) who used it as a term describing perfection in Christian life, and its use was extended by later Greek writers. Both the words "contemplation" and "contemplative", however, were vague in their church use by the twelfth century.

They could have a straightforward intellectual sense: human beings have a "contemplative" facility as they are endowed with reason and understanding; "contemplation", here, simply means "study". At the other extreme, "contemplative" had been given an affective meaning. One general assumption of the second millennium is that meditation involves reasoning, whereas contemplation involves a more instinctive apprehension of whatever mystery or truth is addressed.

We see that Guigo uses the word "contemplation" to refer to something more mystical than academic, more affective than rational, and which he sees as containing elements of blessing, or fruitfulness in prayer life.

As with the word "meditation", the meaning of the word "contemplation" was to undergo more changes and development of meaning later in the history of the Church.

## Concluding reflections

Guigo is a good teacher of sacred reading/praying of scripture (*Lectio divina*) in his "Ladder". The rungs of the ladder are "*Lectio, Meditatio, Oratio, Contemplatio*. These mean Read (scripture), Reflect (Meditate), Pray, Contemplate. Although his third rung is called "Pray", the whole sequence today would be considered a sequence of prayer. Christian Action (*Actio*) is today the usual "fifth rung" for those who follow Guigo's precepts in lay life.

"Meditation" has many meanings, but for Guigo in the twelfth century it would have some overtones of "taking to heart", some of "chewing over" and perhaps some of "study". "Contemplation" likewise has many meanings, but for Guigo it was seen as affective prayer, with overtones of "sharing with God" and of awareness of God and of his blessings.

A focus on Guigo helps our understanding of the long tradition of using scripture for prayer in different ways, many of which are still much in use today.

# Prayers and Devotions from Eastern Monasticism

### The Jesus prayer

This is an important practice in Eastern Christianity, and has become more widespread in the Western Catholic Church in recent years. It belongs to a tradition called *"Hesychasm"*, coming from the Greek word, *"Hesychia"*, meaning "quiet". *Hesychasts* use meditative techniques which don't "hold a conversation" with God. This may be described as nondiscursive prayer (i.e. with no discourse). They also:

i.   have a devotion to Jesus' name,

ii.  have a keen sense of sorrow for sin,

iii. have a discipline of frequent repetition of a phrase containing the word "Jesus" and,

iv.  use the word "Jesus" in imageless prayer to lead to inner silence.

In the 14th century the monk Gregory of Sinai gave the standard phrase as, "Lord Jesus Christ, Son of God, have mercy on me, a sinner". A common way to pray this sentence is,

i.   to breath in on the first phrase, "Lord Jesus Christ",

ii.  to hold breath on the second, "Son of God",

iii. to exhale on the third, "Have mercy on Me" and

iv.  to keep lungs empty on the fourth, "a sinner".

If you are not familiar with this way of praying, try it!

## Icons

The word "icon" is a Greek word meaning "image", and from the days of the early Church images have been an accompaniment to prayer. Early Christian piety often made use of the cross, and such piety may be described as *"stauro-centred"*, i.e. Cross-centred. This tradition continues well-established in most Christian denominations.

Other images are known to have been used from 325 AD, but the flourishing of iconography took place in the Byzantine tradition from 725 to 1204, in the Serbian and Russian traditions from eleventh to the fifteenth centuries, and in the Romanian tradition later still. In the West imagery has made more use of statues. The Eastern tradition has seen icons as an important aid to contemplation.

John Damascene in Jerusalem at the turn of the eighth century, wrote of images of Christ, "But now that he has made himself visible in the flesh and lived with men, I can make an image of what I have seen of God ... and contemplate the glory of God, his face unveiled." Images of Christ include The Baptism and the Transfiguration, The Lamentation at the tomb, The Descent to the Underworld, and The Resurrection. Other common icons are of Mary and the Saints, the Annunciation, Pentecost and the Dormition (called the Assumption in the West). They are used widely in Eastern Churches, and to an increasing degree in the West.

## Concluding reflections

In addition to encouraging the reflective reading of scripture in prayer, the monastic tradition in the East has given us the Jesus prayer and promoted the use of icons. Practising a rhythm of breathing e.g. in the Jesus Prayer, may be beneficial to many. Icons may be a help to reflection and take us deeper into the mysteries of the faith and help us reflect on the life of Christ and the Saints.

# Friars, Prayers & Devotions

## Prayers and devotions ... the mendicant friars

The first Dominicans and Franciscans started a new branch of religious life. They were mendicants (beggars) and saw their mission as in the world, rather than in a monastery. In the thirteenth century Cathars, and other preachers of alternative doctrines to Catholicism, were making converts from former Catholics. Francis in his simple life and Dominic in his preaching won back many to the Catholic Church. They flourished at the time when Church authorities started discouraging scripture reading in the vernacular, and part of the friars' influence was in promoting new forms of prayer through piety and devotions.

## Cribs and Stations

St Francis of Assisi (d. 1226) is credited with producing the first crib, so that people could picture and reflect on God becoming man in Christ (The Incarnation). The Franciscan Order was also mainly responsible for the development of the Stations of the Cross; the practice of following Christ to Calvary aided by depictions of scenes on the way. In the thirteenth century the Church's liturgy was becoming physically more distant from the laity. Churches had long naves, with liturgy going on at one end in a language most could not understand, and the common folk at the other. Francis brought Christ to many in an intelligible way through encouraging "human images" as an aid to prayer.

## The Rosary

The mendicant orders and others encouraged people first to learn the "Our Father" then to repeat this prayer as the friars, or monks in other orders, were praying through the 150 psalms in the liturgy of the hours. This gave rise to "paternoster cords", knotted cords with up to 150 (or some division of 150) knots for people to pray with. In some places the "Our Father" became replaced by the angel's greeting to Our Lady, "Hail, full of grace. The Lord is with you." (giving the then 150 "Hail Mary's" of the three sets of mysteries of the rosary.)

It was the Dominican Order who spread this devotion, which has developed into the rosary we know today. The mid-fifteenth century Dominican, Alanus of

Rupe, was particularly responsible for its growth and spread. Its continued spread and use is witness to very many people finding it a helpful and fruitful way of prayer today.

## THE BODY IN PRAYER

### Dominic's Nine Ways

By the thirteenth century, bodily postures were often seen as part of prayer. The contrast with "prayer" understood being as "words", or "desire", is quite striking. A clear text on using the body in prayer is Dominic's Nine Ways.

The "Nine Ways of Prayer of St Dominic" forms part of a collection of very early Dominican writings, first collected together in Bologna somewhere between 1260 and 1288. The Nine Ways introduces the use of the body in prayer as follows:

> "the way of praying in which the soul uses the members of the body to raise itself more devoutly to God. In this way the soul moving in the body is moved by it. At times it becomes rapt in ecstasy as was St Paul, or is caught up in a rapture of the spirit like the prophet David. Saint Dominic often prayed this way and it is fitting to say something of his method ...".

*The First Way of Prayer (Profound bowing of the head)*

Saint Dominic's first way of prayer was to humble himself before the altar as if Christ, signified by the altar, were truly and personally present and not in symbol alone. He would say with Judith (*Jdt* 9:16) "O Lord, God, the prayer of the humble and the meek hath always pleased thee." "It was through humility that the Canaanite woman and the prodigal son obtained what they desired; as for me, "I am not worthy that Thou shouldst come under my roof" (*Mt* 8:8) for "I have been humbled before you exceedingly, O Lord." (*Ps* 118:107).

*The Second Way of prayer (Prostrating oneself)*

Saint Dominic used to pray by throwing himself outstretched upon the ground, lying on his face. He would feel great remorse in his heart and call to mind those words of the gospel, saying sometimes in a voice loud enough to be heard: "O God be merciful to me, a sinner." (*Lk* 18:13).

*The Third Way of Prayer (Using the discipline, i.e., striking oneself with an object made for this purpose)*

At the end of the prayer which has just been described, Saint Dominic would rise from the ground and give himself the discipline with an iron chain, saying, "This discipline has corrected me unto the end."(*Ps* 17:36).

(N.B. This is NOT current recommended practice of the Dominicans, nor any other order of the Western Church!)

## The Fourth Way of Prayer (Genuflecting, kneeling and rising regularly)

After this, Saint Dominic would remain before the altar or in the chapter room with his gaze fixed on the Crucified One, looking upon Him with perfect attention. He genuflected frequently, again and again. He would continue sometimes from after Compline until midnight.

## The Fifth Way of Prayer (Standing erect before the altar, hands open or closed)

When he was in the convent, our holy father Dominic would sometimes remain before the altar, standing erect without supporting himself or leaning upon anything. Often his hands would be extended before his breast in the manner of an open book.

## The Sixth Way of Prayer (With arms outstretched, making the form of a cross)

Our holy father, Saint Dominic, was also seen to pray standing erect with his hands and arms outstretched forcefully in the form of a cross.

*The Seventh Way of Prayer (Hands together reaching towards heaven)*

While praying he would often reach towards heaven like an arrow which has been shot from a taut bow straight upwards into the sky... He seemed to seek for himself and his brethren something of that transcendent joy which is found in living the beatitudes, praying that each would consider himself truly blessed in extreme poverty, in bitter mourning, in cruel persecutions, in a great hunger and thirst for justice, in anxious mercy towards all.

*The Eighth Way of Prayer (Reading the gospels and other holy texts)*

... Our father quickly withdrew to some solitary place, to his cell or elsewhere and recollected himself in the presence of God. He would sit quietly and, after the sign of the cross, begin to read from a book opened before him. His spirit would then be sweetly aroused as if he heard Our Lord speaking ... he quickly passed upwards from prayer to meditation and from meditation to contemplation ... When he read alone in this solitary fashion, Dominic used to venerate the book, bow to it and kiss it.

*The Ninth Way of Prayer (Praying while walking, fortified by making the sign of the cross)*

Our father, Saint Dominic, observed this mode of prayer while travelling from one country to another. ...Thus withdrawn he would walk and pray; in his meditation he was inflamed and the fire of charity was enkindled. While he prayed it appeared as if he were brushing dust or bothersome flies from his face when he repeatedly fortified himself with the sign of the cross.

## The body in prayer ...other teachings

Earliest pictures of Christians praying often show the person standing with hands uplifted. Gestures, whether kneeling, bowing, prostrating, genuflecting etc. bring with them declarations of a particular kind of relationship.

In the second millennium more attention has been paid to the use of the body in prayer, especially in liturgy, devotion and techniques of meditation. All who pray have bodies, which can at times either get in the way of prayer, or be used to help with prayer. A person's body can cause distractions. Attention to posture, breathing, and other bodily factors can help overcome distractions which arise from the body, and may sometimes help to overcome mental distractions too.

## Distractions

The CCC includes a section entitled "The Battle of Prayer". The first difficulty of prayer to be listed is that of "distraction". To set about hunting down distractions, however, is to "fall into their trap, when all that is necessary is to turn back to our heart" "Distraction hunting" is not strictly an activity of prayer. The succeeding paragraph of the CCC suggests, "In positive terms the battle against the possessive and dominating self requires vigilance, sobriety of heart." We do need to be aware of the problems of distractions, but also to see beyond them.

The Catechism wisely draws our attention to the "Prayer at the Hour of Jesus" and reminds us of the greatness of Jesus' prayer in his passion and death. Jesus was in intense pain and stress. At this time Jesus' body was not free from distractions, his prayer was not part of a routine, his senses were not attuned to prayer. All of these could be seen as providing the worst bodily state for prayer, and yet his prayer was faultless. It is "Always possible to pray" and the developing of good habits for one's body is, in this sense, a secondary consideration, though it is one not to be ignored.

## Development of devotions

Mendicant Orders were key to the growth of devotions and piety, but were by no means the only promoters of such prayers. Important promoters of Marian devotions are Bonaventure (d. 1274) and Bernard of Clairvaux (d. 1153). Later promoters of the rosary include Louis de Montfort (d. 1716). A key figure in the popularity of the Stations of the Cross is Alphonsus of Liguori (1606 - 1787), whose prayers for the Stations are still very popular today.

## Concluding reflections

Dominic's "Nine Ways" is a classical text concerning prayer which gives examples of different ways of using one's body while praying. His nine ways include, **i.** profound bowing, **ii.** prostrations, **iii.** the discipline, **iv.** genuflections, **v.** standing erect before the altar, **vi.** arms outstretched in the sign of the cross, **vii.** hands together reaching towards heaven, **viii.** reading sacred texts, and **ix.** praying while walking and making the sign of the cross.

Our bodies contribute to prayer, but don't dominate it. A good key test for genuine prayer is that it stirs up in the person who prays an ardent charity which moves him/her to collaborate in the mission of the Church and to serve brothers and sisters for the greater glory of God.

This chapter also points to a time in history when devotions began to grow. Through the inspiration and efforts of many teachers of prayer, devotions have flourished in the Church and continue to do so. They use sight, touch and bodily movements to help habits of prayer and to engage with the mysteries of faith.

# Thomas Aquinas
# & his Theology
# of Prayer

## Introduction

*Thomas Aquinas*

Thomas (1225-1274) was born at Roccasecca in Italy. As he grew up he looked to the Church as his vocation, and his family planned that he should join the nearby Benedictine monastery of Monte Cassino. He chose the Dominicans instead and went to Paris, where he was taught by St Albert and was introduced to the philosophy of Aristotle. Albert and Aristotle paved the way for Thomas's major theological work, his *"Summa Theologiae"* often seen as the greatest achievement of systematisation of medieval theology.

He saw the spiritual life as entailing a growth in charity. His spiritual growth model was of three degrees in charity; beginners, proficients and perfects. In his theology of prayer, in terms of "What should I do?" he often suggests one solution in terms of "What should be done to keep God's law", but another deeper solution, for those who wish to be perfect in charity. Because he bases his theology partly on the philosophy of Aristotle, he frequently looks for the "cause" or "causes" of things that happen.

Thomas looks at prayer in the second section of the second part of this *Summa Theologiae*. In this chapter I will look at a selection of his questions and answers of this chapter. The *Summa Theologiae* later became a prominent comprehensive theological text of the Catholic Church. In each article Thomas gives good arguments for and against, then reflects on them together to give his conclusion. "What purpose is served by asking God for things?" asks Thomas or again, "If God is immutable (unchangeable), why try to change his will?" Thomas's theology of petition is most helpful in understanding the Christian activity of asking God for what seems good. He also asks other reasonable questions: "What about Sinners Praying? Do we always pray to God?" etc.

## Thomas' understanding of petition

*Do we ask for something simply because we desire it, or is there a reason to ask?*

In his discussion Thomas takes to pieces the process of requesting things from God. Thomas sees petitionary prayer as a process, so he can look at different parts of it. This process may lead to several possible outcomes. What is asked for may happen. Something else may happen, or nothing may happen.

For Thomas the outcome depends on more than one input. There may be my input (prayer), God's input, or the input of others. Thomas's starting point is to suggest that everything which happens is happening because God wills or allows it. Thomas understands that God is the "primary cause". For Thomas ...God is the primary cause of all things, but petition has the potential to be an important secondary cause, and so it is appropriate for us, as reasoning creatures, to pray from both our desire and our reason when we ask from God.

To understand this, it might be helpful to draw a parallel with human acts which do good things. If I help a little old lady across the road with her shopping, such an act - providing she wants and needs to cross the road - is a good act. The prime cause of all goodness is, of course, God. In that sense the primary cause of her getting across the road is God. I become a secondary cause of what is good by my good actions cooperating with God. God wants me to do good acts. That is the way in which the world usually works. He could waft her across the road with a miraculous wind, but usually he likes me or others to get involved. I am an important "secondary cause" of the little old lady getting across the road.

In a similar way, for Thomas, prayer works as a "secondary cause". God wills good things to happen, but by my free will in asking I play a part in bringing about that good.

I find Thomas's argument to be the most helpful understanding of Christian petition in the history of theology of prayer. It totally acknowledges God's immutability. God does not "have his arm twisted" by prayer. It indicates both privilege and power in human prayer cooperating with God. It shows how prayer can bring good things about. At the same time it acknowledges that God is in charge.

## Is it Appropriate to Pray?

Thomas is clear that any theology of petition must not challenge sound theology of the nature of God. He uses a phrase which he has picked up from St Gregory, "that by asking, men may deserve to receive what God from eternity has disposed to give". Using this he shows the nature of cooperation and freedom between man and God. He envisages that the asking is part of the human/divine partnership which brings about what is good.

*Should our prayer life involve others?*

Thomas argues that when we ask for things, the human norm is to ask those in whose power it is to grant what we ask. He goes on to suggest that we also ask those who might simply help us to get what we want. In the same way when we want to buy something often it is helpful to ask others who have bought the same item previously, or if we wish to travel we ask those who travel frequently on the route that interests us. Such are normal human asking processes. Thomas argues that invoking Saints to pray for us is a normal activity and therefore we pray to saints in the sense that we ask their efforts to be joined with ours to help obtain our requests.

*Should we ask for particular things when we pray?*

Thomas's teaching acknowledges that there are good arguments for "praying generally for God's will or what is good", but also acknowledges that God's revelation in scriptures allows us a more directed prayer for what specific thing seems good to us. (Thomas expects our understanding of what is good to be informed by scripture, reasoning and Church teaching).

*Should we ask God for temporal things in Prayer?*

Augustine, in his letter to Proba had said, "It is lawful to pray for what it is lawful to desire." Thomas agrees with this statement, arguing that it is often appropriate to pray for "things".

*Should we pray for other people?*

Thomas here uses poor references, but his arguments are still good. We pray for others out of charity. We pray better as a body. God's blessings given to one person help others too. Needing other's prayers helps our humility.

*Should we pray for our enemies?*

Thomas argues that we are bound to pray for our enemies in the same way that we are bound to love them.

> "A man must be prepared to love his enemy even in the individual and to help him in a case of necessity, or if his enemy should beg his forgiveness. But to love one's enemies absolutely in the individual, and to assist them, is an act of perfection."

> "In like manner it is a matter of obligation that we should not exclude our enemies from the general prayers which we offer up for others: but it is a matter of perfection, and not of obligation, to pray for them individually, except in certain special cases."

When Thomas talks about "a matter of perfection", he does so within a framework or the virtue of charity/love. For Thomas the fullness of charity is the route to perfection in spiritual life. This is why he refers to the deeper levels of charity when discussing praying for individual enemies. In addition to this he suggests that general prayers for all, should include enemies along with everyone else.

*Do the Saints in heaven pray for us?*
Thomas argues here, as he often does in the *Summa*, from his understanding of charity. The Saints, according to his argument have the greatest human charity, and therefore they pray for us powerfully.

*Ought prayer to be vocal?*
Thomas sees public prayer (liturgy) as always needing to be vocal, and advises private prayer to be vocal too, for our benefit, unless the spoken words distract us.

*Do sinners obtain anything from God by praying?*
Thomas argues in brief that when a sinner prays for what is good, and prays piously, God hears him out of mercy, but not when he prays for evil.

## Concluding reflections

Prayer acts to help bring about the good things willed by God. i.e. God is the primary cause of all that is good (the first cause), but also gives us the role and privilege of bringing good things about by prayer. It is appropriate in prayer, in addition to prayer to God, to ask Saints to join their petitions with ours. It is appropriate to pray generally for God's will, but also specifically for things that seem to us to be good. Charity encourages us to pray not only for ourselves, but for others, too. It is good to pray in a body as well as individually. Many prayers together have a greater power than individuals' prayer. Thanking God for individual graces brings benefit to many. Finding that we need the prayers of "the less perfect" stops us from getting too proud.

# Ignatius of Loyola: Prayer, Choice & God

## Introduction

### Ignatius of Loyola

I gnatius (1491-1556) began his adult life as a Spanish courtier. In 1521 he suffered leg wounds in battle and during his recovery had a profound conversion. While recuperating Ignatius was bed-bound and so was confined to a life more of reflection than action.

## Consolation and desolation

Ignatius discovered that reflecting on the events in the life of Christ and the Saints gave him a more lasting peace and contentment than reflecting on secular life. This sense of peace/contentment he called "consolation", the opposite, "desolation". He developed the *"Spiritual Exercises"*, which contain several different forms of prayer, to help others recognise such consolation and grow to God through it. This chapter introduces some of his teachings.

## Spiritual Exercises

He went on to found the Society of Jesus (Jesuits) and to use his own understanding of awareness of Christ in retreats for others. The text of the *Spiritual Exercises* comprises a series of guidelines for the retreat-giver to help retreatants to encounter Christ in their retreats. They are neither a textbook on spiritual life, nor a series of spiritual reflections. They were written for use by a retreat-master leading a retreatant through the spiritual journey of the Exercises. Their influence however, is profound.

The Spiritual Exercises are usually split into four weeks:

**Week One** - includes directions on Examination of Conscience, Confession, Holy Communion etc., but the central mysteries it reflects on are those of good and evil. These meditations consider the sin of the fallen angels, the sin of Adam, reflections on the cross of Christ, and the angels and saints in heaven, as well as our attraction to mortal sin and the place of Hell. Ignatius' model for spiritual growth is very much within the sacraments and the liturgy, especially the Mass and the sacrament of Reconciliation.

**Week Two** - has as its centre "The Kingdom of Christ". It brings with it a sense of working with Christ to build his kingdom. Several exercises (*Ex* 136-148) compare life beneath the standard of Christ with life beneath the standard of Lucifer, and the attractions of each. There is a call to be aware of, and indifferent to, any attractions which are not of Christ himself. It helps to expose any divided loyalties in the person who undertakes the *Spiritual Exercises*.

The second week is also very centred on the Trinity and the persons of the Trinity. In the *"Rules for thinking with the Church"*, Ignatius values Christ's promise to guide his Church, and seeks to instil trust and confidence in the Church as a body, both now, and throughout its living Tradition.

**Week Three** - seeks to deepen the immersion in the mysteries of Christ, especially his passion, crucifixion, death and burial in the grave. The retreatant is called to deep compassion, sharing with Christ in his suffering and experiencing, in some way, Christ's death. The retreatant longs for Christ's resurrection. As with previous weeks, both the intellectual and affective aspects of human life have to be addressed.

**Week Four** - brings with it joyful reflection on the Resurrection, Christ's divinity, and the personal commitment to Christ in one's life.

Ignatius's spirituality is more comprehensive than most. It is *Sacramental*, *Trinitarian*, *Christocentric* (centred on Christ), *Ecclesial* (to do with being "Church"), and Scriptural. It works on the person's intellect, emotions, desires, fantasies, and will.

## Prayer Structure

The norm in Ignatius' instructions for prayer is that each time of prayer will have three components:

**i.** The Preparation

**ii.** The Body of the Prayer and

**iii.** The *Colloquy* (which means "conversation")

## Preparation

Before entering into the body of the prayer Ignatius usually recommends a short time to be spent considering what is to be done in the prayer time as a whole, and asking for the grace to carry out the particular exercise which the prayer involves. He may recommend setting the mind at rest and using a posture which doesn't distract the body too much. The typical prayer here asks that all intentions, operations and acts be directed to the service and praise of God's divine majesty.

## The central meditation

Ignatius starts many of his Exercises in prayer with some form of meditation, often what is known as discursive meditation, where the subject matter is mulled over.

## Colloquy

A colloquy is a familiar intimate conversation, as between close family members about what has happened during the previous two components of the prayer. We mentally discuss our prayer with God.

## Is there an Ignatian prayer method?

The teachings of Ignatius give many methods, but the method most widely known of these is sometimes simply known as the "Ignatian Method", which draws from several strands in the Exercises. A good exposition of it is found in Bede Frost's book. I give here a brief outline of this method:

i.  Choose a scripture passage for meditation and read through it the evening before you intend to use it, selecting several points for meditation. (Use two or three questions to "ask" the text, Who? What? Where? By what aids? Why? How?

When? From Whom? With What love? With What Fruit?).

ii. At this time you may also ask: "Who speaks or acts? Where and with whom?" (Such questions help form the "Composition of Place")

iii. Sleep on it!

iv. Rise, dress briskly, adore God, and imagine your Composition of Place. Imagine, too Him whom you will meet there.

v. Raise the mind and heart to God while praying an "Our Father".

vi. Make a gesture of reverence/self –abasement.

vii. Start the Meditation Proper! ...Recall the subjects chosen ...Picture yourself in the scene.

viii. Ask briefly of the Lord for knowledge so that we may love him more dearly and follow him more nearly.

ix. (Body of the Meditation) Use the memory, understanding and will on the subject. The memory brings forward the subject, the understanding reflects on it, trying to be taught by it. This leads to personal questions "What have I done concerning this to date? What shall I do from today? What obstacles may I encounter? What steps should I take? The will is exercised in the resolves which come from these questions.

x.  This leads to desire and petition, which are expressed in the colloquy and bring forth prayer and action in one's life.

The CCC quotes Ignatius on Contemplation when it says "Contemplation also turns its gaze on the mysteries of the life of Christ. Thus it learns the 'interior knowledge of our Lord', the more to love him and follow him."

*Meditation using the senses*

Many of Ignatius's Exercises and suggestions make use of imagination and the senses. This requires use of the imagination of our senses (sight, sound touch etc.) as we "enter" the scriptural scene.

## Does Ignatius teach other prayer methods?

Yes he does, many! He mentions three particular methods of prayer in the appendix to the Exercises (Ex 238-260). I want to look here only at the first of these.

*First Method*

The first Method of Prayer uses and reflects on the Ten Commandments, and on the Seven Deadly Sins, on the Three Powers of the Soul and on the Five Bodily Senses. Each are reflected on with God's help. This method of prayer is meant to help the soul to prepare itself for God's grace by using the above lists. It is intended to ensure that whatever prayer follows may be acceptable. It enables the perception of God's grace and goodness in one's own life.

It is one of several occasions where Ignatius encourages people to use their senses in an *Examen*, i.e., a reflection on their own life in the light of the gospel. Unlike most examinations of conscience, Ignatius's *examens* use all the human faculties at one's disposal in the reflection (It is not simply a case of "Have I kept rules?"). He also looks at virtues in addition to sins.

Ignatius uses and values the words of all the standard prayers of his time, especially the Our Father and the Hail Mary. He recognises the benefits of bodily posture and breathing (as in the Jesus Prayer).

The expectation that all those who pray would be familiar with the Seven deadly sins, with their contrasting virtues, with the three powers of the soul, show the influence which theology has had on the Church in the second millennium. The structures of virtue and vice have been codified and these understandings have become, for Ignatius and his followers, an integral part of the life of prayer.

## Concluding reflections

Ignatius of Loyola used his own experience of reflecting on Christ's life to discern what leads to God. His *Spiritual Exercises* were written so that others could be directed in similar ways of meditation and reflection to find God's will for their lives. Ignatius's spirituality is more comprehensive than most. It works on the person's intellect, emotions, desires, fantasies, and will. It uses reflection on the created world to show and experience God. It encourages us to think with the Church as well as use reason and imagination to be open to God's Spirit. Ignatius' methods of prayer call on us to use reason, will, imagination, fantasy, and imaginative construction of place. By the use of these we experience scriptural scenes deeply and are taught by them. He suggests reflection on categories of sins and virtues in addition to scriptural scenes. His *examens* help retreatants to see themselves in God's eyes and not only to repent, but to grow in good habits and in virtue.

# Teresa of Avila & John of the Cross: Carmelite Prayer

## Introduction

The Carmelite order lacks a founder, but traces its origins back to Mount Carmel, where its early hermit fathers sought solitude, prayer and contemplation. Many generations followed. St Albert gave the order an eremitic rule in approximately 1210, and, although today few of the order are true hermits, solitude and prayer still maintain a place in the charism of the Carmelites. The first convent of nuns appeared in the Low Countries in 1452. Female convents spread rapidly through France, Italy and Spain.

---

### Teresa of Avila and John of the Cross

Teresa was born in Avila in 1515. She and John of the Cross (1542-1591) were to become the great reformers of the order. They are also great teachers on the mystical life and on prayer. Their influence

---

has remained strong in the Church from that time on. Teresa entered the Convent of the Incarnation in 1533. The life there was not highly disciplined. In 1555 she underwent a conversion and committed herself to a life of spiritual perfection. In 1562 she founded the convent of St Joseph, seeking a stricter way of following the rule. She was helped by St John of the Cross in her efforts to reform the order, though both of them met strong and often violent opposition to their labours.

## Teresa's writing

Teresa's central works are the *"Book of her Life"* (or *"Life"*) (autobiographical), her *"Foundations"*, *"The Interior Castle"* and the *"Way of Perfection"*. Teresa was not a "trained theologian" and quotes no theological writers in her books, although she had been influenced by St Augustine's Confessions and took that as something of a model for her *"Life"*. Her books were written to try to express what she subjectively learned from her own spiritual life.

Building on models of *"Spiritual life as a journey"* (based on Origen, but developed further in the Middle Ages), Teresa and John of the Cross described their understanding of a growing, developing relationship with God which encompasses will, emotions and intellect. In so doing, the understandings and use of the words "prayer", "meditation" and "contemplation" have changed and have broadened. New sub-categories of these words have also come into use.

Teresa had profound religious experiences. She gave new meanings to some pre-existing words describing prayer, and used new phrases to try to express her experiences. These are not always precise, nor, perhaps as clear as one would wish, but have been found useful to many people. She also sought to express what she learnt from her experiences using allegory, and part of Teresa's gift to the Church is in her allegorical pictures of the spiritual life. A brief introduction to her terminology and allegory is called for in this chapter.

## Terminology

Before looking at Teresa's and John's writings it is good to recap and develop the background of terms which would have been present and probably familiar to them in Sixteenth-century Spain.

Origen's three starting points of a Christian's Spiritual journey, based on the books attributed to Solomon, (Proverbs, Ecclesiastes and Song of Songs) had given rise, by the Middle Ages, to two similar classification systems, each having three points of reference. (Teresa is most unlikely to be aware of Origen's texts.)

Growth in Charity has been mentioned already in the chapter on Thomas Aquinas. The three-stage classification of growth in holiness used by Thomas Aquinas and the Dominican school was centred on charity. In the Christian life one sought to move from being a beginner, to being proficient, then perfect in charity. The expectation was that deepening charity would move us on in our prayer lives. Like Origen, Thomas had an expectation of initial stages being concerned with freedom from sin, later stages as deepening our lives in the mysteries of Christ and his Church, and the final stages bringing closer union with God, in addition to deepening the virtues.

The mystical tradition more common in Spain at Teresa and John's time favoured instead the three-stage terminology developed by the Franciscan, St Bonaventure [d. 1274] and many later authors. Again it had three focal points. These were described as *purgative*, *illuminative* and *unitive* ways.

The understanding was that in the first zeal of conversion, the Christian would have the majority of his/her energies focussed on freedom from sin: a moral conversion. Sin would be rooted-out, hence the term "purgative".

The next main focus of energies (N.B. The desire for freedom from sin would still be very much present) would be the desire to grow in understanding, and to seek the revelation of God, hence "Illuminative". This is initial growing in the depth of the mysteries of God.

The third stage was that of deepest union, in the image of the love-poetry of the Song of Songs, hence "Unitive".

Along with the concepts of spiritual growth came concepts of the types of prayer which accompanied these stages of spiritual growth.

The tradition of writing about "prayer" in terms of its New Testament roots of "asking for things" was not strong in Teresa's day. The growth and development of religious communities who were committed to mental prayer resulted in many books being written for contemplative religious communities rather than for laity. Most commonly, the word "prayer" was by now used in books to describe a broad range of activities of mind and heart in relation to God, rather than vocal petition.

## Meditation and contemplation

"Meditation" in Sixteenth-century Spain often meant discursive meditation, perhaps using a specific method such as that of St Ignatius, but it could also be used to refer any type of mental prayer. Likewise "Contemplation" had passed from meaning any type of "sacred study" and was now more likely to mean some type of mental prayer where apprehension of God was not achieved as an answer to our imagination, or reason, but primarily as a gift from God.

Terminology grew concerning the perceived starting-point of the prayer (Did it seem to have human or divine origins?). For both meditation and contemplation various writers taught that the impulse of prayer could subjectively seem to come from ourselves, in which case it was often called **active** (in mental prayer often called **acquired** meditation or contemplation). Alternately efforts in prayer may subjectively seem to emanate from God. These prayers were often described as **passive**, or when describing meditation or contemplation, **infused**.

The prayer of **quiet**, which in the Eastern Church was associated with *Hesychasm*, had in the Western Church slightly more diffuse meanings, but referred to mental prayer in which imagination and reason were not being actively engaged by the person praying.

## Teresa's "Classical" prayer definition

In chapter 8 of the *"Life"* we read:

> "I hope in the mercy of God, whom no one has ever taken for a friend without being rewarded; and mental prayer, in my view, is nothing but friendly intercourse, and frequent solitary converse, with Him who we know loves us."

From this prayer definition it is easy to see the genesis of the prayer definition of the later Carmelite, St Thérèse of Lisieux: "For me, prayer is a surge of the heart; it is a simple look turned toward heaven, it is a cry of recognition and of love, embracing both trial and joy."

## Teresa's Garden

A good place to start looking at Teresa's prayer terminology is in her "garden". In Chapter eleven of her "Life", she tries to outline her simple idea of what happens in the soul that seeks God.

Teresa starts by encouraging her reader to imagine making, in themselves, a garden for God's pleasure, full of human virtues, but currently weedy and barren. She continues: Let us now see how this garden is to be watered, that we may understand what we have to do: how much trouble it will cost us, whether the gain be greater than the trouble, or how long a time it will take us. It seems to me that the garden may be watered in four ways:

i. by water taken out of a well, which is very laborious; or

ii. with water raised by means of an engine and buckets, drawn by a windlass - I have drawn it this way sometimes - it is a less troublesome way than the first, and gives more water; or

**iii.** by a stream or brook, whereby the garden is watered in a much better way - for the soil is more thoroughly saturated, and there is no necessity to water it so often, and the labour of the gardener is much less; or

**iv.** by showers of rain, when our Lord Himself waters it, without labour on our part - and this way is incomparably better than all the others of which I have spoken.

It should be noted that in Spain gardens need water or they dry up. One's mindset needs to be attuned away from the English world of lawns which in a damp year can survive without any extra water whatsoever. Think instead "water means life! No watering means shrivelling and dying!" This indicates the essential nature of Teresa's images.

Teresa decides to draw up the balance-sheet of what effort is needed and whether it is all worthwhile: "Let us now see how this garden is to be watered, that we may understand what we have to do: how much trouble it will cost us, whether the gain be greater than the trouble, or how long a time it will take us..." Her entire approach is very "matter of fact".

**i.** Start with "Spiritual Weeding". Root up the weeds and plant "good herbs", i.e., root out habits of sin and firmly plant sound habits of prayer, virtue, sacraments and love.

ii. Lots of "bucket work". This is a dispiriting stage of effort, i.e., acquired prayer of a hard-work-meditation type.

iii. Gradually the hard work changes as easier methods emerge by using the windlass. This represents a later stage of prayer, still mainly acquired - there is much personal effort - but with more fruit.

iv. Next, divert the stream to water your plants. The nature of the prayer changes subjectively; the flow seems to be coming from God rather than from you.

v. Finally it rains! ... No effort at all seems to be required, i.e., there is total infused prayer, perfect contemplation.

Teresa later wrote the "Interior Castle", in which she imagines progressing from one room of mental prayer to the next, until she reaches the ultimate in the seventh room. Outside are loathsome creatures, inside is the true path.

The first three rooms (*moradas*) are active prayer (the person does most of the work) Room one is vocal prayer, although the soul is still much attached to things of this earth. Room two marks the start of discursive meditation, which has much dryness, but the one praying progresses from reasoning towards love. The third room is one of acquired recollection, where there is much awareness of God. All attention is centred on God.

Room four marks the first stage of infused prayer, which Teresa calls the prayer of quiet. The will is filled with divine love, but memory and imagination may still disturb the soul. Room five is a deeper infused prayer, the prayer of union, which may vary in intensity, but the soul finds itself in God and God in itself.

For rooms six and seven Teresa uses bridal imagery. The symbols are mystical espousal and marriage. Both Song of Songs imagery and Jesus' call to complete unity, ("as he is united to the Father", *Jn* 17:22-23), are called to mind. It is the deepest union. For Teresa it was sometimes accompanied by ecstasy.

Teresa's terminology varies slightly with her different books. The book of her Life gives the impression that progress is from prayer of recollection to prayer of quiet, to "sleep of the powers". The latter term implies that memory, understanding and will are unable to be used in prayer at this stage. From there the path leads to the prayer of union and ecstasy. The Interior Castle, written twelve years later, has the sequence: recollection, quiet, union (with or without ecstasy) and spiritual marriage.

Teresa's terminology and her teaching, based on awareness of her own spiritual life do not spring from the traditional theology. They are descriptive, rather than analytical terms. They have been invaluable in guiding others who attempt mental prayer and come across the same experiences. They are often seen as part of a greater "Carmelite Spirituality" which includes the writings of John of the Cross and others. Thérèse of Lisieux too, as she reflects in prayer on the centrality of love in small things, makes a third central writer. All three are doctors of the Church, recognised great teachers on prayer and the spiritual life.

## John of the Cross

John's spiritual life, too, involved the emotions and can be said, in today's terms, to have been centred on a passionate love for Our Lord, especially Our Lord crucified.

John's major works are his poems and his commentaries on them (*The Ascent of Mount Carmel*, *The Dark Night*, *The Living Flame of Love* and *The Spiritual Counsels*). He has other works which build on these also. John has a great love for the "Our Father" but also reflects on finding God in places of beauty, in the wilderness and on mountains.

He, like Teresa invests much of his time and energy in mental prayer, and calls others to do so too. The CCC quotes his *"Maxims and Counsels"* in which he sees contemplation as "silent love." In his *"Special Counsels to a Religious"* he describes mental prayer as the "sustenance of your soul" and says "Never give up on mental prayer, and should you find dryness and difficulty, persevere in it for this very reason. God often desires to see what love your soul has, and love is not tried by ease and satisfaction." He also gives detailed specific instructions relating to when, for instance, one should discontinue discursive meditation and pass on to contemplative meditation. He is a spiritual guide or director without equal for the contemplative person praying in the Christian tradition. He and Teresa share much of the same spiritual vision, but she paints clear broad pictures, whereas he gives detailed personal guidance on individual points of progress.

## Concluding reflections

Teresa is a great teacher of mental prayer, whose teaching is based on her own experiences. Teresa's central definition of prayer and all her teachings are down-to-earth using non-theological language. Teresa was acquainted with some descriptions of different types of mental prayer, but uses her own terms of recollection, quiet, union (with or without ecstasy) and the spiritual marriage. These have passed into general usage thanks to her writing and teaching. Teresa's teachings on prayer go hand-in-hand with the spiritual teachings of St John of the Cross, her fellow reformer of the Carmelite order, and also provide the background for the more recent St Thérèse of Lisieux.

## Epilogue

When lawyers construct a good argument for use in court, they do their job well. What should motivate them, however, is not simply the desire to produce words which are effective in persuading others to accept their case, but the thirst for justice. When poets describe aspects of our world and our lives in flowing words which move us to look deeper, or understand, or appreciate something more fully, they do their job well. At the heart of a good poet, however, is the perception of beauty or the awareness of great truths. The most important purpose of conversation between people is always found in a deeper intention. When individuals develop a love of conversation for its own sake rather than a love of those with whom they hold that conversation, or a desire to share and express what is important, then there is something lacking.

The Dominican writer, Vincent McNabb, had a horror of those who prayed from a love of prayer and not from love of God. It is a sentiment I share. Prayer may be beautiful, profound, and it may subjectively seem to be personally fulfilling, but it must not become an end in itself. It is a mistake to put prayer itself at the centre of our lives. God must be that centre. Prayer is a means to an end. We must not forget that other activities, those flowing from Christian virtues, and the living-out of every Christian vocation are means to that same end. God is that end we seek.

Prayer is a channel to God. Because of this and because of its many fruits it has tremendous worth. Our awareness of the place of prayer in our lives varies. When we pray we are often motivated in an immediate way, by habit. The techniques involved in our prayer, too, are often habitual. Indeed good habits are central to regular prayer. What may motivate us at a deeper level may be fear, hope, love, or other passions.

Prayer is one of God's gifts to be treasured, regardless of how it comes about. Prayer is a necessary gift from God which enables our direct communication, and intimacy, with God in the Trinity. Without it our faith becomes lifeless, and our life lacks direction, lacks faith and hope.

The different chapters of this book show that prayer has many different aspects. Some images show prayer helping us to grow in our relationship with God. Some seek to highlight different aspects of our humanity, (reason, will, emotions, body, habits, personal and community dimensions of life) in our communication with God. Words to do with prayer have been understood in different ways as time progresses, but the essential nature of prayer, of communication with God, endures to eternity.

We have inherited a rich tradition of prayer-life. Throughout Christian history the circumstances of the day and the inspirations of God have moulded the prayer of individuals and communities. Prayer-life may, in our own lives develop or change, but in the Church no good way of prayer ever dies out, and none is completely new. God does not change. Human nature does not change. We have a God-shaped hole within us. St Augustine long ago recognised this with his words to God, "You have made us for yourself and our hearts are restless until they find their rest in you."

Each time we offer a prayer our restless hearts grow closer to the one we love.

## Further Reading

*A Catechism of Christian Doctrine* - revised edition, CTS 1971.

*Tertullian on Prayer*, Aide Inter Monasteres (AIM) trans. Justice, C. (O. Cist) 1991 Printed Our Lady of Bethlehem Abbey, Portglenone, Antrim.

Greer, R (trans) Origen, *An Exhortation to Martyrdom, Prayer and selected works*, Classics of Western Spirituality series Paulist Press New York 1979.

Hand, T. A., *Augustine on Prayer*, Catholic Book Publishing Co. New York 1986.

Colledge, E & Walshe, J., *The Ladder of Monks and Twelve Meditations by Guigo II*, Mowbray, London & Oxford 1978.

Tugwell, S., *Albert & Thomas, Selected Writings*, Classics of Western Spirituality Series, Paulist Press, New York 1988.

Munitiz, J. A. & Endean, P (trans & ed.) *Saint Ignatius of Loyola, Personal Writings*, Penguin Classics, London 1996.

Frost, Bede, *The Art of Mental prayer*, The Alban Press, London 1988 Chap 1.

Kavanaugh, K (trans.), *The Collected Works of St Teresa of Avila*, (Especially Vol. 1), ICS Publications, Washington, 2002.

Pourrat, P., *Christian Spirituality III*, Burns, Oates & Washbourne, London 1927.

Aumann, J., *Christian Spirituality in the Catholic Tradition*, Sheed & Ward, London 1985.